This note book belongs to :

____

Date:

____

Made in the USA
Monee, IL
20 December 2020

54056626R00059